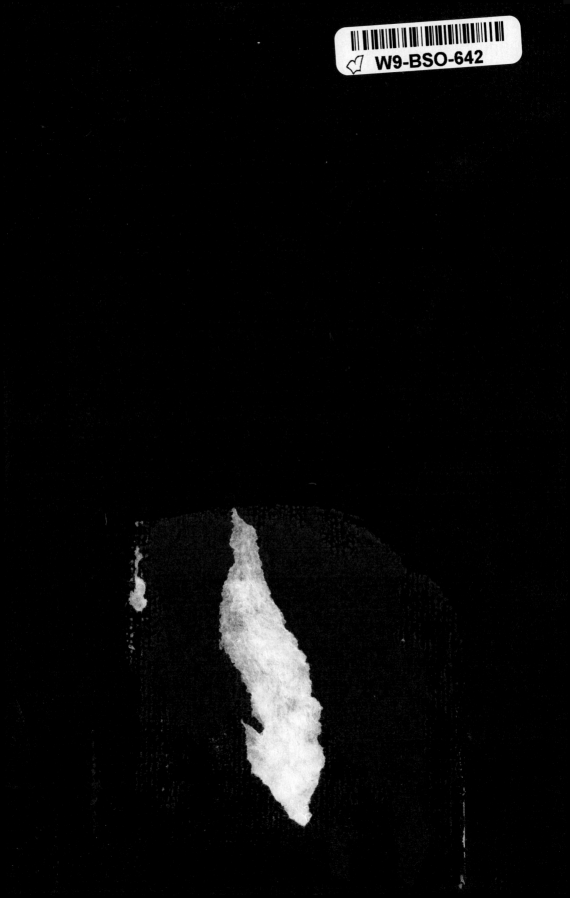

BOOKS BY Robert Penn Warren

John Brown: The Making of a Martyr

Thirty-six Poems

Night Rider

Eleven Poems on the Same Theme

At Heaven's Gate

Selected Poems, 1923–1943

All the King's Men

Blackberry Winter

The Circus in the Attic

World Enough and Time

Brother to Dragons

Band of Angels

Segregation: The Inner Conflict in the South

Promises: Poems 1954–1956

Selected Essays

The Cave

All the King's Men (play)

You, Emperors, and Others: Poems 1957–1960

The Legacy of the Civil War

Wilderness

Flood

Who Speaks for the Negro?

Selected Poems: New and Old 1923–1966

Incarnations: Poems 1966–1968

INCARNATIONS

POEMS

1966–1968

Robert Penn Warren

INCARNATIONS

POEMS 1966–1968

RANDOM HOUSE   NEW YORK

FIRST PRINTING

Copyright © 1967, 1968 by Robert Penn Warren

All rights reserved under International and Pan-American Copyright Conventions.

Published in the United States by Random House, Inc., New York,

and simultaneously in Canada by Random House of Canada Limited, Toronto.

Some of the poems in this collection have appeared in Encounter, Northwest
Review, Harper's, The Reporter, Saturday Review, The New York Review of Books,
The University of Denver Quarterly, Yale Review, and The New Yorker.

Library of Congress Catalog Card Number: 68–28529

Manufactured in the United States of America

Design by Betty Anderson

TO John Palmer

Yet now our flesh is as the flesh of our brethren.
—NEHEMIAH 5.5

John Henry said to the Captain, "A man ain't nuthin but a man."   —A FOLK BALLAD

CONTENTS

III · ENCLAVES

I · ISLAND OF SUMMER

＊ *This symbol is used to indicate a space between sections of a poem wherever such spaces are lost in pagination.*

1

WHAT DAY IS

In Pliny, *Phoenice.* Phoenicians,
Of course. Before that, Celts.
Rome, in the end, as always:
A handful of coins, a late emperor.
Hewn stone, footings for what?
Irrigation, but now not easy
To trace a flume-line.

                    Later,
Monks, Moors, murderers,
The Mediterranean flotsam, not
Excluding the English, they cut
Down olives, plucked vines up, burnt
The chateau.

                    All day, cicadas,
At the foot of infinity, like
A tree, saw. The sawdust
Of that incessant effort,
Like filings of brass, sun-brilliant,
Heaps up at the tree-foot. That
Is what day is.

                    Do not
Look too long at the sea, for
That brightness will rinse out your eyeballs.

They will go gray as dead moons.

WHERE THE SLOW FIG'S PURPLE SLOTH

Where the slow fig's purple sloth
Swells, I sit and meditate the
Nature of the soul, the fig exposes,
To the blaze of afternoon, one haunch
As purple-black as Africa, a single
Leaf the rest screens, but through it, light
Burns, and for the fig's bliss
The sun dies, the sun
Has died forever—far, oh far—
For the fig's bliss, thus.

            The air
Is motionless, and the fig,
Motionless in that imperial and blunt
Languor of glut, swells, and inward
The fibers relax like a sigh in that
Hot darkness, go soft, the air
Is gold.

       When you
Split the fig, you will see
Lifting from the coarse and purple seed, its
Flesh like flame, purer
Than blood.

       It fills
The darkening room with light.

NATURAL HISTORY

Many have died here, but few
Have names, it is like the world, bodies
Have been eaten by dogs, gulls, rodents, ants,
And fish, and Messire Jean le Maingre,
He struck them, and they fled.

                              Et les Sarrasins
se retirèrent en un isle qui est devant
le dict chastel—

                but little good that, for
The *Maréchal* was hot on them, and

                               des leurs
y perdirent plus de quatre cent hommes,
que morts, que affolez,

                    and the root
Of the laurel has profited, the leaf
Of the live-oak achieves a new luster, the mouth
Of the mullet is agape, and my ten-year-old son,
In the island dump, finds a helmet, Nazi—from left
To right, entering at the temple, small and
Perfectly round at the point of entry, neat, but
At egress large, raw, exploding outward, desperate for
Light, air, and openness after
The hot enclosure and intense dark of
That brief transit: this

The track of the missile. Death
Came quick, for history,
Like nature, may have mercy,
Though only by accident. Neither
Has tears.

        But at dusk
From the next island, from its pad at
Le centre de recherche d'engins spéciaux, the rocket
Rises, the track of fume now feathers white—spins out, oh whiter—
Rises beyond the earth's shadow, in
Full light aspires. Then,
With no sound, the expected explosion. The glitters
Of flame fall, like shreds of bright foil, ice-bright, from
A Christmas tree, die in earth's shadow, but
The feathers of fume yet hang high, dissolve
White in that last light. The technicians
Now go to dinner.

        Beauty
Is the fume-track of necessity. This thought
Is therapeutic.

        If, after several
Applications, you do not find
Relief, consult your family physician.

RIDDLE IN THE GARDEN

My mind is intact, but the shapes
of the world change, the peach
has released the bough and at last
makes full confession, its *pudeur*
has departed like peach-fuzz wiped off, and

We now know how the hot sweet-
ness of flesh and the juice-dark hug
the rough peach-pit, we know its most
suicidal yearnings, it wants
to suffer extremely, it

Loves God, and I warn you, do not
touch that plum, it will burn you, a blister
will be on your finger, and you will
put the finger to your lips for relief—oh, do
be careful not to break that soft

Gray bulge of fruit-skin of blister, for
exposing that inwardness will
increase your pain, for you
are part of the world. You think
I am speaking in riddles. But I am not, for

The world means only itself.

PAUL VALÉRY STOOD ON THE CLIFF AND CONFRONTED THE FURIOUS ENERGIES OF NATURE

Where dust gritty as
    Hot sand was hurled by
    Sea-wind on the cliff-track
    To burnish the holly-leaf, he

Walked, and white the far sail
    Heeled now to windward, and white
    Cat's-paws up the channel flicked.
    He paused to look, and far down,

Surf, on the Pointe du Cognet,
    Boomed, and clawed white,
    Like vine incessant, up
    That glitter and lattice of air.

Far down, far down, below
    The stone where his foot hung, a gull
    Wheeled white in the flame of
    Air. The white wing scythed

The bright stalks of altitude
    Down, they were cut at the root,
    And the sky keeps falling down,
    Forever it falls down with

    *

A clatter like glass, or delight,
    And his head, like a drum, throbs,
    His eyes, they fly away,
    They scream like gulls, and

Over Africa burn all night,
    But Time is not time, therefore
    His breath stops in his throat
    And he stands on the cliff, his white

Panama hat in hand,
    For he is Monsieur le Poète,
    Paul Valéry is his name,
    On a promenade by the sea, so

He sways high against the blue sky,
    While in the bright intricacies
    Of wind, his mind, like a leaf,
    Turns. In the sun, it glitters.

6

TREASURE HUNT

Hunt, hunt again. If you do not find it, you
Will die. But I tell you this much, it
Is not under the stone at the foot
Of the garden, nor by the wall by the fig tree.
I tell you this much to save you trouble, for I
Have looked, I know. But hurry, for

The terror is, all promises are kept.

Even happiness.

7

MOONRISE

The moon, eastward and over
The ridge and rock-blackness, rears.
From the widening throat of the valley,
Light, like a bugle-blast,
Silver, pours at us. We are,
In that silence, stunned.

                    The faces
Of clients on the café *terrasse*
From shadow lift up. From the shadow
Of sockets, their eyes yearn, and
The faces, in that light, are
Washed white as bone.

                    Some,
However, have shown more judgment.
They loll in the shadow of laurel.

The air is heavy with blossom.

We wait. We do not even
Know the names of one another.

8

MYTH ON MEDITERRANEAN BEACH:
APHRODITE AS LOGOS

From left to right, she leads the eye
Across the blaze-brightness of sea and sky

That is the background of her transit.

Commanded thus, from left to right,
As by a line of print on that bright

Blankness, the eye will follow, but

There is no line, the eye follows only
That one word moving, it moves in lonely

And absolute arrogance across the blank

Page of the world, the word burns, she is
The word, all faces turn. Look!—this

Is what she is: old hunchback in bikini.

A contraption of angles and bulges, an old
Robot with pince-nez and hair dyed gold,

✳

She heaves along beneath the hump.

The breasts hang down like saddle-bags,
To balance the hump the belly sags,

And under the belly-bulge, the flowers

Of the gee-string garland the private parts.
She grinds along by fits and starts

Beside the margin of the sea,

Past children and sand-castles and
The lovers strewn along the sand.

Her pince-nez glitter like contempt

For all delusion, and the French lad
Who exhibitionistically had

Been fondling the American college girl

*

Loses his interest. Ignoring him,
The hunchback stares at the horizon rim,

Then slowly, as compulsion grows,

She foots the first frail lace of foam
That is the threshold of her lost home,

And moved by memory in the blood,

Enters that vast indifferency
Of perfection that we call the sea.

How long, how long, she lingers there

She may not know, somnambulist
In that realm where no Time may subsist,

But in the end will again feel

The need to rise and re-enact
The miracle of the human fact.

She lifts her head, looks toward the shore.

※

She moves toward us, abstract and slow,
And watching, we feel the slow knowledge grow—

How from the breasts the sea recedes,

How the great-gashed navel's cup
Pours forth the ichor that had filled it up,

How the wavelets sink to seek, and seek,

Then languishing, sink to lave the knees,
And lower, to kiss the feet, as these

Find the firm ground where they must go.

The last foam crisps about the feet.
She shivers, smiles. She stands complete

In Botticellian parody.

Bearing her luck upon her back,
She turns now to take the lifeward track,

And lover by lover, on she moves

✳

Toward her own truth, and does not stop.
Each foot stumps flat with the big toe up,

But under the heel, the damp-packed sand,

With that compression, like glory glows,
And glory attends her as she goes.

In rapture now she heaves along,

The pince-nez glitter at her eyes,
The flowers wreathe her moving thighs,

For she treads the track the blessèd know

To a shore far lonelier than this
Where waits her apotheosis.

She passes the lovers, one by one,

And passing, draws their dreams away,
And leaves them naked to the day.

9

MISTRAL AT NIGHT

Heat, and cold curdle of wind-thrust, moonlight
To tatters torn, on night-blue the tetter
Of cloud-scud, and in shadow
Of laurel the clash of the dry leaf: and that,
In the moment of long remission when
But a single gust stirs, is
In your sleep, and is as
Unforgettable as what is most deeply
Forgotten—and that, oh,
Will be the last thing remembered, at last, in
That instant before remembering is over. But what
Is it? You must wait

To find out. Hold your breath, count to ten. The world
Is like wind, and the leaves clash. This knowledge
Is the beginning of joy. I

Tell you this as explicitly as I can, for
Some day you may find the information
Of crucial importance.

10
THE IVY

The ivy assaults the wall. The ivy
    says: "I will pull you down." Time
    is nothing to the ivy. The ivy

Does not sweat at night, for like the sea
    it dreams a single dream, it
    is its own dream. Therefore,

Peace is the dream's name. The wall
    is stone, and all night the stone,
    where no stars may come, dreams.

Night comes. You sleep. What is your dream?

11

WHERE PURPLES NOW THE FIG

Where purples now the fig, flame in
 Its inmost flesh, a leaf hangs
 Down, and on it, gull-droppings, white
 As chalk, show, for the sun has

Burned all white, for the sun, it would
 Burn our bones to chalk—yes, keep
 Them covered, oh flesh, oh sweet
 Integument, oh frail, depart not

And leave me thus exposed, like Truth.

THE RED MULLET

The fig flames inward on the bough, and I,
Deep where the great mullet, red, lounges in
Black shadow of the shoal, have come. Where no light may

Come, he the great one, like flame, burns, and I
Have met him, eye to eye, the lower jaw horn,
Outthrust, arched down at the corners, merciless as

Genghis, motionless and mogul, and the eye of
The mullet is round, bulging, ringed like a target
In gold, vision is armor, he sees and does not

Forgive. The mullet has looked me in the eye, and forgiven
Nothing. At night I fear suffocation, is there
Enough air in the world for us all, therefore I

Swim much, dive deep to develop my lung-case, I am
Familiar with the agony of will in the deep place. Blood
Thickens as oxygen fails. Oh, mullet, thy flame

Burns in the shadow of the black shoal.

13

A PLACE WHERE NOTHING IS

I have been in a place where
nothing is, it is not
silence, for there are voices, not
emptiness, for there is
a great fullness, it is
populated with nothingness, nothing-
ness presses on the ribs like
elbows angry, and the lump
of nothingness sticks
in the throat like the hard
phlegm, and if, in that dark,
you cough, there is, in that
land of nothingness, no
echo, for the dark has
no walls, or if there is echo,
it is, whatever the original
sound, a laugh. A lamp
by each bed burns, but
gives no light.

        Earlier,
I have warned you not to look
too long at the brightness of
the sea, but now—yes—
I retract my words, for
the brightness of that nothing-
ness which is the sea is
not nothingness, but is
like the inestimable sea of

Nothingness Plotinus dreamed.

14

MASTS AT DAWN

Past second cock-crow yacht masts in the harbor go slowly white.

No light in the east yet, but the stars show a certain fatigue.
They withdraw into a new distance, have discovered our
                                                unworthiness. It is long since

The owl, in the dark eucalyptus, dire and melodious, last called, and

Long since the moon sank and the English
Finished fornicating in their ketches. In the evening
                                                there was a strong swell.

Red died the sun, but at dark wind rose easterly, white
                        sea nagged the black harbor headland.

When there is a strong swell, you may, if you surrender to it, experience
A sense, in the act, of mystic unity with that rhythm. Your peace
                                                is the sea's will.

But now no motion, the bay-face is glossy in darkness, like

An old window pane flat on black ground by the wall, near
                                                the ash heap. It neither
Receives nor gives light. Now is the hour when the sea

❊

Sinks into meditation. It doubts its own mission. The drowned cat

That on the evening swell had kept nudging the piles of
                                        the pier and had seemed
To want to climb out and lick itself dry, now floats free. On that
                                surface a slight convexity only, it is like

An eyelid, in darkness, closed. You must learn to accept the
                                                kiss of fate, for

The masts go white slow, as light, like dew, from darkness
Condenses on them, on oiled wood, on metal. Dew whitens in darkness.

I lie in my bed and think how, in darkness, the masts go white.

The sound of the engine of the first fishing dory dies seaward. Soon
In the inland glen wakes the dawn-dove. We must try

To love so well the world that we may believe, in the end, in God.

15

THE LEAF

[A]

Here the fig lets down the leaf, the leaf
Of the fig five fingers has, the fingers
Are broad, spatulate, stupid,
Ill-formed, and innocent—but of a hand, and the hand,

To hide me from the blaze of the wide world, drops,
Shamefast, down. I am
What is to be concealed. I lurk
In the shadow of the fig. Stop.
Go no further. This is the place.

To this spot I bring my grief.
Human grief is the obscenity to be hidden by the leaf.

[B]

We have undergone ourselves, therefore
What more is to be done for Truth's sake? I

Have watched the deployment of ants, I
Have conferred with the flaming mullet in a deep place.

Near the nesting place of the hawk, among
Snag-rock, high on the cliff, I have seen
The clutter of annual bones, of hare, vole, bird, white
As chalk from sun and season, frail
As the dry grass stem. On that

High place of stone I have lain down, the sun
Beat, the small exacerbation
Of dry bones was what my back, shirtless and bare, knew. I saw

The hawk shudder in the high sky, he shudders
To hold position in the blazing wind, in relation to
The firmament, he shudders and the world is a metaphor, his eye
Sees, white, the flicker of hare-scut, the movement of vole.

Distance is nothing, there is no solution, I
Have opened my mouth to the wind of the world like wine, I wanted
To taste what the world is, wind dried up

*

The live saliva of my tongue, my tongue
Was like a dry leaf in my mouth.

Destiny is what you experience, that
Is its name and definition, and is your name, for

The wide world lets down the hand in shame:
Here is the human shadow, there, of the wide world, the flame.

[c]

The world is fruitful. In this heat
The plum, black yet bough-bound, bursts, and the gold ooze is,
Of bees, joy, the gold ooze has striven
Outward, it wants again to be of
The goldness of air and—oh—innocent. The grape
Weakens at the juncture of the stem. The world

Is fruitful, and I, too,
In that I am the father
Of my father's father's father. I,
Of my father, have set the teeth on edge. But
By what grape? I have cried out in the night.

From a further garden, from the shade of another tree,
My father's voice, in the moment when the cicada
                                    ceases, has called to me.

[D]

The voice blesses me for the only
Gift I have given: *teeth set on edge.*

In the momentary silence of the cicada,
I can hear the appalling speed,
In space beyond stars, of
Light. It is

A sound like wind.

II · INTERNAL INJURIES

1

To Brainard and Frances Cheney

KEEP THAT MORPHINE MOVING, CAP

Oh, in the pen, oh, in the pen,
The cans, they have no doors, therefore
I saw him, head bent in that primordial
Prayer, head grizzled, and the sweat,
To the gray cement, dropped. It dripped,
And each drop glittered as it fell,
For in the pen, oh, in the pen,
The cans, they have no doors.

Each drop upon that gray cement
Exploded like a star, and the Warden,
I heard the Warden saying, "Jake—
You know we're pulling for you, Jake,"
And I saw that face lift and explode
In whiteness like a star, for oh!—
Oh, in the pen, yes, in the pen,
The cans, they have no doors.

A black hole opened in that white
That was the star-exploding face,
And words came out, the words came out,
"Jest keep that morphine moving, Cap,
And me, I'll tough it through,"
Who had toughed it through nigh forty years,
And couldn't now remember why
He had cut her throat that night, and so
Come to the pen, here to the pen,
Where cans, they have no doors,

✳

31

And where he sits, while deep inside,
Inside his gut, inside his gut,
The pumpkin grows and grows, and only
In such a posture humped, can he
Hold tight his gut, and half believe,
Like you or me, like you or me,
That the truth will not be true.—Oh, Warden,

Keep that morphine moving, for
All night beneath that blazing bulb,
Bright drop by drop, from the soaked hair, sweat
Drips, and each drop, on the gray cement,
Explodes like a star. Listen to that
Small sound, and let us, too, keep pulling
For him, like we all ought to, who,
When truth at last is true, must try,
Like him, to tough it through—but oh!—
Not in the pen, not in the pen,
Where cans, they have no doors.

2

TOMORROW MORNING

In the morning the rivers will blaze up blue like sulphur.
Even the maps will shrivel black in their own heat,
And metaphors will scream in the shared glory of their referents.
Truth will embrace you with tentacles like an octopus. It
Will suck your blood through a thousand suction-cups, and
The sun utter the intolerable trill of a flame-martyred canary.

Does this suggest the beginning of a new life for us all?

Or is it only, as I have heard an eminent physician remark,
A characteristic phase at the threshold of the final narcosis?

3

WET HAIR: IF NOW HIS MOTHER SHOULD COME

If out of a dire suspicion
She hadn't touched his hair and
Found it yet damp at the roots, she might
Have forgiven the fact he was late,
With supper near over now, and the lamp

On the table already lighted, and shadows
Bigger than people and blacker than niggers swinging
On the board walls of the kitchen, one kid,
The youngest, already asleep,
The head at the edge of
The plate, and tighter than glue
In that hot night, one cheek
To the checked oil-cloth table cover, and grease
Gone gray on the forks—yes, if

She hadn't then touched his hair,
She might never have guessed how he'd been in
That durn creek again, and then lied,
And so might never have fetched him that
Awful whack. His face

In the lamplight was white. She

Stood there and heard how,
Maniacal and incessant,
Out in the dark, the
Insects of summer tore

The night to shreds. She
Stood there and tried to think she
Was somebody else. But
Wasn't, so

Put him to bed without supper.

What if tonight when
Again the insects of summer
Are tearing the night to shreds, she
Should come to this room where under the blazing
Bulb, sweat drips, and each drop,
On that gray cement, explodes like
A star? What if she
Should touch his head and now
Find the hair wetter than ever?

I do not think that now she
Would fetch him that awful
Whack—even if

Again he had come late to supper,
Then lied, to boot.

NIGHT: THE MOTEL DOWN THE ROAD FROM THE PEN

Now in the cheap motel, I lie, and
Belly-up, the dead catfish slides
All night glimmering down the river
That is black and glossy as
Old oil bleeding soundlessly
From the crank-case. Look! the stars

Are there, they shine, and the river
Knows their white names as it flows,
And white in starlight the white belly
Glimmers down the magisterial
Moving night the river is.

In this motel, I lie and sweat.
It is summer, it is summer.

The river moves. It does not stop.
It, like night, is going somewhere.

It is going, somewhere.

5

WHERE THEY COME TO WAIT FOR THE BODY:
A GHOST STORY

This is the cheap motel where
They come to wait for the body if they
Are white, and have three dollars to spare,

Which is tough if you had to scrape up to pay
Private for the undertaker because you
Hope he'll make things look better some way,

But won't, for with twenty-three hundred volts gone through,
The customer's not John Barrymore,
And the face he's got will just have to do

Him on out, so load the finished product and go, for
You've long since done with your crying, and now
It's like it all happened long back, or

To somebody else. But referring to Jake, how
Could they schedule delivery, it might be next week,
Or might, if things broke right, be even tomorrow,

But who gives a damn how the cheese, so to speak,
Gets sliced, for nobody's waiting to haul
Jake back to any home cross-roads or creek,

And there's nobody here, nobody at all,
Who knows his name even, but me, and I know
Only the Jake part, but I've got a call

✳

In for five A.M., for I'm due to blow
At half-past, but if he'd be checked out and ready,
If that's not too early for him, he can go

With me, and we roll, and his eyes stare moody
Down a road all different from the last time he passed,
And the new slab whirls at him white now and steady,

And what he might recognize snaps by so fast
That hill and stream and field all blur
To a misty glitter, till at last

He shifts on his hams and his stiff hands stir
On his knees, and he says: "That bluff—thar 'tis!
Jest let me off thar, thank you kindly, sir."

And so he drops off at the creek where that bluff is,
And the shadow of woods spills down to the bone-
White slab, and with back to the screech and whizz

Of the traffic, he stands, like he was alone
And noise no different from silence, his face set
Woodsward and hillsward, then sudden, he's gone,

And me, I'm gone too, as I flog the U-Drive-It
Toward Nashville, where faces of friends, some dead, gleam,
And where, when the time comes, you grab the jet.

6

NIGHT IS PERSONAL

Night is personal. Day is public. Day
Is like a pair of pants you can buy anywhere, and do.

When you are through with day you hang it up like pants on
The back of a chair, and it glows all night in the motel room, but not

Enough to keep you awake. Jake is awake. Oh, Warden,
Keep that morphine moving, for we are all

One flesh, and back in your office, in the dark, the telephone
Is thinking up something to say, it is going to say

It does not love you, for night is each man's legend, and there is no joy
Without some pain. Jake is meditating his joy. He sweats. Oh, Warden,

Keep that morphine moving, for I feel something
Soft as feathers whispering in me, and

Corpuscles grind in your own blood-stream, like gravel
In a freshet, and by this sign know that a congress

Of comets will be convened screaming, they will comb their
Long hair with blue fingers cold as ice, their tears are precious, therefore

*

My head explodes with flowers like a gangster's funeral, but
                                        all this racket won't
Matter, for Jake is awake anyway. Oh, Warden, keep
                                that morphine moving, for

When you get home tonight your wife will be weeping. She
Will not know why, for in the multiple eye of the spider, the world bleeds

Many times over, the spider is hairy like a Jewish Jesus, it
                                        is soft like a peach
Mercilessly bruised, you have tasted the blood of the spider, and

It smiles, it knows. Jake is awake. Oh, Warden,
Keep that morphine moving, for your father is not really dead, he

Is trying to get out of that box he thinks you put him in, and
                                on the floor by your bed, in the dark,
Your old dog, like conscience, sighs, the tail feebly thumps, it wants

To be friends again, it will forgive you even if now you
Do take it to the vet, for now is the time, it has suffered
                                        enough. Oh, Warden,

Keep that morphine moving, for we've had a frightful summer, sweat
Stings my eyes, salt pills do no good, forest fires rage
                                at night in the mountains. Warden,

❊

Things have got to change around here. Jake's case is simply
One of many. An investigation is coming, I warn you. And anyway,

Night is personal, night is personal. There are many nights, Warden,
And you have no reason to think that you are above the Law.

7

DAWN

Owl, owl, stop calling from the swamp, let
Old orange peel and condoms and
That dead catfish, belly white, and
Whitely, whitely, the shed petals
Of catalpa—let all, all,
Slide whitely down the sliding darkness
That the river is, let stars
Dip dawnward down the un-owled air, and sweat
Dry on the sheet.

             But
Stars now assume the last brightness, it
Is not yet dawn. Dawn will, it
Is logical to postulate, though not
Certain, come, and the sun then,
Above the horizon, burst
Like a blast of buckshot through
A stained-glass window, for

It is summer, it is summer.

Forgive us, this day, our joy.

Far off, a red tractor is crossing the black field.
Iron crushes the last dawn-tangle of ground mist.

Forgive us—oh, give us!—our joy.

1

THE EVENT

Nigger: as if it were not
Enough to be old, and a woman, to be
Poor, having a sizeable hole (as
I can plainly see, you being flat on the ground) in
The sole of a shoe (the right one), enough to be

Alone (your daughter off in
Detroit, in three years no letter, your son
Upriver, at least now you know
Where he is, and no friends), enough to be

Fired (as you have just today
Been, and unfair to boot, for
That durn Jew-lady—there wasn't no way
To know it was you that opened that there durn
Purse, just picking on you on account of
Your complexion), enough to be

Yourself (yes, after sixty-eight
Years, just to have to be
What you are, yeah, look
In the mirror, that
Is you, and when did you
Pray last), enough to be,

Merely to be—Jesus,
Wouldn't just *being* be enough without
Having to have the pee (quite

Literally) knocked out of
You by a 1957 yellow Cadillac driven by
A spic, and him
From New Jersey?

Why couldn't it of at least been a white man?

2

THE SCREAM

The scream comes as regular
As a metronome. Twelve beats
For period of scream, twelve
For period of non-scream, there
Must be some sort of clockwork
Inside you to account for such
Perfection, perhaps you have always
And altogether been clockwork, but
Not realizing its perfection, I
Had thought you merely human.

I apologize for the error, but
It was, under the circumstances,
Only natural.

        Pneumatic hammers
Are at work somewhere. In the period
Of non-scream, they seem merely a part of the silence.

3

HER HAT

They are tearing down Penn Station,
Through which joy and sorrow passed,

But against the bright blue May-sky,
In the dazzle and sun-blast,

I can see one cornice swimming
High above the hoarding where

Sidewalk superintendents turn now
From their duties and at you stare,

While I, sitting in my taxi,
Watch them watching you, for I,

Ashamed of their insensitiveness,
Am no Peeping Tom with my

Own face pressed directly to the
Window of your pain to peer

Deep in your inward darkness, waiting,
With slack-jawed and spit-wet leer,

*

For what darkling gleam, and spasm,
Visceral and pure, like love.

Look! your hat's right under a truck wheel.
It's lucky traffic can't yet move.

Somewhere—oh, somewhere above the city—a jet is prowling the sky.

4

THE ONLY TROUBLE

The only trouble was, you got up
This morning on the wrong side of the bed, and of
Your life. First, you put the wrong shoe on the right
Foot, or vice versa, and next
You quarreled with your husband. No—
You merely remembered a quarrel you had with him before he
Up and died, or did he merely blow, and never
Was rightly your husband, nohow.

                              Defect of attention
Is defect of character, and now
The scream floats up, and up, like a
Soap bubble, it is enormous, it glitters
Above the city, it is as big as the city,
And on its bottom side all the city is
Accurately reflected, making allowance
For curvature, upside-down, iridescent as
A dream, oh pale!

              If children were here now,
They would clap their hands for joy.

                              But,
No matter, for in stunning soundlessness, it
Explodes, and over the city a bright mist
Descends of—microscopically—spit.

THE JET MUST BE HUNTING FOR SOMETHING

One cop holds the spic delicately between thumb and forefinger.
It is as though he did not want to get a white glove dirty.

The jet prowls the sky and Penn Station looks bombed-out.

The spic has blood over one eye. He had tried to run away.
He will not try again, and in that knowledge, his face is
                    as calm as congealing bacon grease.

Three construction workers come out from behind the hoarding.

The two cops are not even talking to each other, and in spite of
The disturbance you are so metronomically creating, ignore
                    you. They are doing their duty.

The jet prowls. I do not know what it is hunting for.

The three construction workers are looking at you like a technical
Problem. I look at them. One looks at his watch. For everything
                    there is a season.

How long since last I heard birdsong in the flowery hedgerows of France?

✻

Just now, when I looked at you, I had the distinct impression
                    that you were staring me straight in the eye, and
Who wants to be a piece of white paper filed for eternity on
                              the sharp point of a filing spindle?

The orange-colored helmets of the construction workers
                              bloom brilliant as zinnias.

When you were a child in Georgia, a lard-can of zinnias
                              bloomed by the little cabin door.
Your mother had planted them in the lard-can. People
                              call zinnias nigger-flowers.

Nobody wants to be a piece of white paper filed in the dark
                    on the point of a black-enameled spindle forever.

The jet is so far off there is no sound, not even the sizzle
                    it makes as it sears the utmost edges of air.
It prowls the edge of distance like the raw edge of experience.
                                        Oh, reality!

I do not know what the jet is hunting for. It must
                              be hunting for something.

6
BE SOMETHING ELSE

Be something else, be something
    That is not what it is, for
    Being what it is, it is
    Too absolute to be.

If you insist on being
    What you are, how can we
    Ever love you, we
    Cannot love what is—

By which I mean a thing that
    Totally is and therefore
    Is absolute, for we
    Know that the absolute is

Delusion, and that Truth lives
    Only in relation—oh!
    We love you, we truly
    Do, and 'we love the

World, but we know
    We cannot love others unless
    We learn how to love
    Ourselves properly, and we truly

Want to love you, but

For God's sake stop that yelling!

7

THE WORLD IS A PARABLE

I must hurry, I must go somewhere
Where you are not, where you
Will never be, I
Must go somewhere where
Nothing is real, for only
Nothingness is real and is
A sea of light. The world
Is a parable and we are
The meaning. The traffic
Begins to move, and meaning
In my guts blooms like
A begonia, I dare not
Pronounce its name. —Oh, driver!
For God's sake catch that light, for

There comes a time for us all when we want to begin a new life.

All mythologies recognize that fact.

8

DRIVER, DRIVER

Driver, driver, hurry now—
Yes, driver, listen now, I
Must change the address, I want to go to

A place where nothing is the same.
My guts are full of chyme and chyle, of Time and bile, my head
Of visions, I do not even know what the pancreas is for, what,

Driver, driver, is it for?
Tell me, driver, tell me true, for
The traffic begins to move, and that fool ambulance at last,

Screaming, screaming, now arrives.
Jack-hammers are trying, trying, they
Are trying to tell me something, they speak in code.

Driver, do you know the code?
Tat-tat-tat—my head is full of
The code, like Truth or a migraine, and those men in orange helmets,

They must know it, they must know,
For *tat-tat*, they make the hammers go, and
So must know the message, know the secret names and all the
                                    slithery functions of

*

All those fat slick slimy things that
Are so like a tub full of those things you
Would find in a vat in the back room of a butcher shop, but
wouldn't eat, but

Are not that, for they are you.
Driver, do you truly, truly,
Know what flesh is, and if it is, as some people say, really sacred?

Driver, there's an awful glitter in the air. What is the weather forecast?

III · ENCLAVES

1

THE FARING

Once over the water, to you borne brightly,
Wind off the North Sea cold but
Heat-streaked with summer and honed by the dazzle
Of sun, and the Channel boat banging
The chop like a shire-horse on cobbles—thus I,
Riding the spume-flash, by gull cries ringed,
Came.

Came, and the harbor slid smooth like an oil-slick.
It was the gray city, but the gray roof-slates
Sang blue in the sun, and the sea-cliffs,
Eastward, swung in that blue wind. I came thus,
And I, unseen, saw. Saw
You,

And you, at the pier edge, face lifted seaward
And toward that abstract of distance that I
Yet was and felt myself to be, stood. Wind
Tugged your hair. It tangled that brightness. Over
Your breast wind tautened the blue cloth, your skirt
Whipped, the bare legs were brown. Steel
Rang on steel. Shouts
Rose in that language.
Later,

The quiet place. Roses. Yellow. We came there, wind
Down now, sea slopping the rocks, slow, sun low and
Sea graying, but roses were yellow, climbing
The wall, it was stone. That last light

Came gilding a track across the gray water from westward.
It came leveling in to finger the roses. One
Petal, yellow, fell, slow.

At the foot of the gray stone, like light, it lay.
High beyond roses, a gull, in the last light, hung.

The sea kept slopping the rocks, slow.

2

THE ENCLAVE

Out of the silence, the saying, into
The silence, the said, thus
Silence, in timelessness, gives forth
Time, and receives it again, and I lie

In darkness and hear the wind off the sea heave.
Off the sea, it uncoils. Landward, it leans,
And at the first cock-crow, snatches that cry
From the cock's throat, the cry,
In the dark, like gold blood flung, is scattered. How

May I know the true nature of Time, if
Deep now in darkness that glittering enclave
I dream, hangs? It shines. Another
Wind blows there, the sea-cliffs,
Far in that blue wind, swing. Wind

Lifts the brightening of hair.

1

SKIERS

To Baudouin and Annie de Moustier

With the motion of angels, out of
Snow-spume and swirl of gold mist, they
Emerge to the positive sun. At
That great height, small on that whiteness,
With the color of birds or of angels,
They swoop, sway, descend, and descending,
Cry their bright bird-cries, pure
In the sweet desolation of distance.
They slowly enlarge to our eyes. Now

On the flat where the whiteness is
Trodden and mud-streaked, not birds now,
Nor angels even, they stand. They

Are awkward, not yet well adjusted
To this world, new and strange, of Time and
Contingency, who now are only
Human. They smile. The human

Face has its own beauty.

2

FOG

White, white, luminous but
Blind—fog on the
Mountain, and the mountains

Gone, they are not here,
And the sky gone. My foot
Is set on what I

Do not see. Light rises
From the cold incandescence of snow
Not seen, and the world, in blindness,

Glows. Distance is
Obscenity. All, all
Is here, no other where.

The heart, in this silence, beats.

[B]

Heart—oh, contextless—how
Can you, hung in this
Blank mufflement of white

Brightness, now know
What you are? Fog,
At my knees, coils, my nostrils

Receive the luminous blindness,
And deeper, deeper, it, with the
Cold gleam of fox-fire among

The intricate secrets of
The lungs, enters, an eye
Screams in the belly. The eye

Sees the substance of body dissolving.

[c]

At fog-height, unseen,
A crow calls, the call,
On the hem of silence, is only

A tatter of cold contempt, then
Is gone. Yes, try to remember
An act that once you thought worthy.

The body's brags are put
To sleep—all, all. What
Is the locus of the soul?

What, in such absoluteness,
Can be prayed for? Oh, crow,
Come back, I would hear your voice:

That much, at least, in this whiteness.

ROBERT PENN WARREN

was born in Guthrie, Kentucky, in 1905. After graduating summa cum laude *from Vanderbilt University (1925), he received a master's degree from the University of California (1927), did graduate work at Yale University (1927–28) and then at Oxford as a Rhodes Scholar (B. Litt., 1930).*

A list of Mr. Warren's books appears in the front of this volume. The variety of forms is extraordinary, including eight novels, eight volumes of poetry, short stories, a play, critical essays, a biography, a historical essay, and two studies of race relations in America. This body of work has been published in a period of thirty-nine years—a period during which Mr. Warren also had an active career as a professor of English. He is now a member of the faculty of Yale University.

All the King's Men *(1946) was awarded the Pulitzer Prize for fiction.* Promises *(1957) won the Pulitzer Prize for poetry, the Edna St. Vincent Millay Prize of the Poetry Society of America, and the National Book Award. In 1944 Mr. Warren occupied the Chair of Poetry of the Library of Congress. In 1959 he was elected to the American Academy of Arts and Letters. In 1967 he received the Bollingen Prize in Poetry for* Selected Poems: New and Old, 1923–1966.

Mr. Warren lives in Connecticut with his wife, Eleanor Clark (author of Rome and a Villa *and* The Oysters of Locmariaquer), *and their two children, Rosanna and Gabriel.*